Legendary Warriors

by Adrienne Lee

Consultant:
Barbara J. Fox
Professor Emerita
North Carolina State University

CAPSTONE PRESS
a capstone imprint

Blazers Books are published by Capstone Press,
1710 Roe Crest Drive, North Mankato, Minnesota 56003
www.capstonepub.com

Library of Congress Cataloging-in-Publication Data
Lee, Adrienne, 1981–
Aztec warriors / by Adrienne Lee.
pages cm. — (Blazers books. Legendary warriors)
Includes index.
Summary: "Describes the lives of Aztec warriors, including their daily life, weapons, and fighting techniques"—Provided by publisher.
ISBN 978-1-4765-3117-5 (library binding)
ISBN 978-1-4765-3375-9 (ebook PDF)
1. Aztecs—Wars—Juvenile literature. 2. Indian weapons—Mexico—Juvenile literature. 3. Aztecs—Juvenile literature. I. Title.
F1219.76.W37L44 2014
972—dc23   2013010311

Editorial Credits
Megan Peterson and Mandy Robbins, editors; Kyle Grenz, designer; Wanda Winch, media researcher; Jennifer Walker, production specialist

Photo Credits
The Bridgeman Art Library: © Look and Learn/Private Collection/Angus McBride, 26-27; Capstone: Carl Lyons, 5, 6 (all), 8-9, 12, 13, 25, 28; Courtesy of Christopher Morton, cover (bottom); Getty Images: National Geographic Stock/Felipe Davalos, 14-15, Ned M. Seidler, 23; Image from Aztec Warrior AD 1325-1521, by John Pohl, © Osprey Publishing Ltd., 17, 20, Image from Blood and Gold - The Americas At War, by Rochard Bodley Scott, Graham Briggs and Rudy Scott Nelson, © Osprey Publishing Ltd., 11; iStockphoto: Dorling Kindersley, 18; Shutterstock: bigredlynx, back cover (sword), Bill Perry, 29, Irafael, cover (background): young-miniatures.com: Young, B. Song, cover (Aztec warrior)

Printed in the United States of America in Stevens Point, Wisconsin.
032013   007227WZF13

Table of Contents

The Valley
of Mexico....................4

Fierce Warriors............10

Aztec Weapons
and Armor 16

A Proud Culture
Fades Away 24

Glossary..................30

Read More 31

Internet Sites............31

Index 32

THE VALLEY OF MEXICO

Long ago, Aztec warriors charged onto the battlefields of Central America. They fought to keep the Aztec empire safe and gain new lands.

IT'S A FACT

The best warriors became emperors **of the Aztec Empire.**

Central America—the narrow strip of land at the southern end of North America

empire—a large territory ruled by a powerful leader

emperor—a male ruler of a country or group of countries

Aztecs wrote down their history in books called codices. Much of what we know about the Aztecs comes from these books.

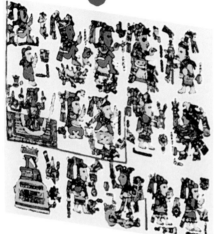

In 1325 the Mexica Indians built the city of Tenochtitlan (teh-NOCHE-teet-lan) in the Valley of Mexico. They joined with three other **city-states** in 1428 to rule the valley. Together these people were called the Aztecs.

◀ **The market in the city of Tlateloco was the largest in the region.**

city-state—a self-governing community including a town and its surrounding territory

The Aztecs took control of every
city in the valley. Each city had to
pay the Aztecs in food, weapons,
and jewelry.

IT'S A FACT

Forms of payment included strange items, such as feathers and rubber balls.

FIERCE WARRIORS

All Aztec boys trained for war. The best fighters entered military groups called **societies**. Most society warriors came from **noble** families. These families owned land and ran the government.

IT'S A FACT

All Aztec men, both farmers and trained warriors, had to fight when called to war.

society—a group that shares the same laws and customs

noble—an upper-class person of high rank

Some Aztec girls went to school. Most were trained to cook, sew, and care for children.

The sons of emperors and nobles went to special schools. These schools trained them to be priests, leaders, or warriors. Experienced warriors taught the boys how to use weapons.

↑ **an Aztec priest**

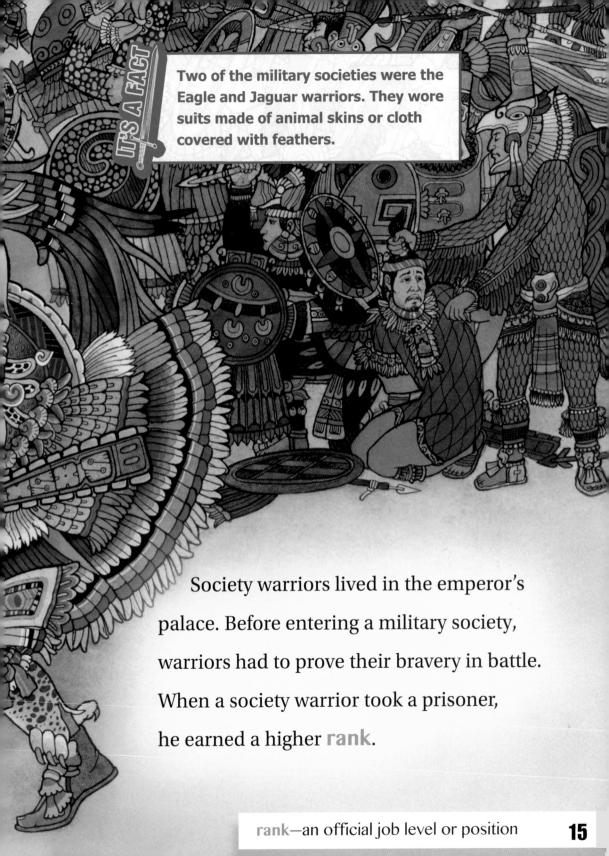

Two of the military societies were the Eagle and Jaguar warriors. They wore suits made of animal skins or cloth covered with feathers.

Society warriors lived in the emperor's palace. Before entering a military society, warriors had to prove their bravery in battle. When a society warrior took a prisoner, he earned a higher **rank**.

rank—an official job level or position

AZTEC WEAPONS AND ARMOR

Aztec warriors fought with bows and arrows. The bows were about 5 feet (1.5 meters) long. The best **archers** could shoot two or three arrows at once.

Aztec warriors carried woven slings. Fighters used the slings to launch stones at their enemies.

archer—a person who shoots a bow and arrow

IT'S A FACT

Aztec men only carried weapons during war. During peacetime, weapons were stored in armories.

Warriors shot sharp darts as enemies drew closer. They used wooden dart throwers called atlatls (AHT-laht-els). A hook held the dart in place as the warrior swung his arm. Darts flew faster than arrows.

armory—a place where weapons are stored

← an Aztec using an atlatl

The emperor and society warriors led attacks. They fought with swords and spears. Swords were about 3 feet (1 m) long. Spears were about 6 feet (2 m) long.

IT'S A FACT

As many as 200,000 Aztec warriors attacked and captured some cities.

↑ Aztec leaders make a battle plan.

IT'S A FACT

Archers and dart throwers stayed behind the front lines. They never fought hand to hand.

Most Aztec warriors didn't wear armor. Warriors wore helmets made of wood or bone. They also carried bamboo, wooden, or copper shields.

A PROUD CULTURE FADES AWAY

In 1519 Spanish explorer Hernán Cortés sailed to Mexico. He hoped to defeat the Aztecs and take their gold. Aztec emperor Montezuma invited the Spaniards into Tenochtitlan. But the Spaniards took him prisoner.

No one knows why Montezuma did not fight the Spanish at first. Some experts believe Montezuma thought Cortés was a god.

In July 1520 the Aztecs chased the Spanish out of Tenochtitlan. Cortés and his men surrounded the city. Supplies of food and water could not reach the city. Many Aztecs starved to death.

The Spanish also spread the
smallpox disease to the Aztecs.
It killed 25 percent of the Aztecs.

The Aztecs **surrendered** to Cortés on August 13, 1521. Cortés destroyed Tenochtitlan. He built a new city called Mexico City in the same place.

surrender—to give up or admit defeat

Today historians continue to find pieces of Tenochtitlan. They learn about what life was like for the Aztecs.

GLOSSARY

archer (AHR-chur)—a person who shoots a bow and arrow

armory (AR-muh-ree)—a place where weapons are stored

Central America (SEN-truhl uh-MER-i-kuh)—the narrow strip of land at the southern end of North America; Central America borders Mexico on the north end and Colombia on the south end

city-state (SI-tee-STAYT)—a self-governing community including a town and its surrounding territory

emperor (EM-puhr-uhr)—a male ruler of a country or group of countries

empire (EM-pire)—a large territory ruled by a powerful leader

noble (NOH-buhl)—an upper-class person of high rank

rank (RANGK)—an official job level or position

society (suh-SYE-uh-tee)—a group that shares the same laws and customs; Aztec warriors in military societies lived in the emperor's palace

surrender (suh-REN-dur)—to give up or admit defeat

READ MORE

Clint, Marc. *Aztec Warriors.* Torque: History's Greatest Warriors. Minneapolis: Bellwether Media, 2012.

Ganeri, Anita. *How the Aztecs Lived.* Life in Ancient Times. New York: Gareth Stevens, 2011.

Guillain, Charlotte. *Aztec Warriors.* Fierce Fighters. Chicago: Raintree, 2010.

INTERNET SITES

FactHound offers a safe, fun way to find Internet sites related to this book. All of the sites on FactHound have been researched by our staff.

Here's all you do:

Visit *www.facthound.com*

Type in this code: 9781476531175

archers, 16, 22

armor, 22

armories, 19

codices, 6

Cortés, Hernán, 24, 25, 26, 28

dart throwers, 19, 22

emperors, 4, 13, 15, 21, 24

Montezuma, 24, 25

nobles, 10, 13

priests, 13

schools, 12, 13

society warriors, 10, 15, 21, 22

Tenochtitlan, 7, 24, 26, 28, 29

weapons, 8, 13, 16–21, 22